Life and Death

PAIRED:

Two people who stood at a crossroads. Businessman Wes Moore met a convicted murderer of about the same age, with the same name, and from the same state—and tried to figure out where their paths had split. Gang member Maria Reyes faced a difficult choice: betray her friends and family or put an innocent man in jail.

"[For] those of us who live in the most precarious places in this country, our destinies can be determined by a single stumble down the wrong path, or a tentative step down the right one."

Wes Moore

"I was raised in gangs. My father was in a gang; my brother was in a gang; my uncles and cousins were in gangs. I didn't know anything else. I thought drive-bys, drug deals, and beatings were normal."

Maria Reyes

Photographs © 2012: Alamy Images/Gianni Muratore: 62; Freedom Writers Foundation: 94 (Mark Eastman), back cover right, 3 right, 56, 100; Getty Images: 24 (Michael Appleton/NY Daily News Archive), 86 (Anne Frank Fonds - Basel/Anne Frank House), cover (Glowimages), back cover left, 3 left (Jason Kempin), 52 (Joe Kohen/IAVA), 54 (PM Images); Kevin B. Moore: 10, 34; Landov, LLC/Pete Marovich/MCT: 38; Media Bakery/Nancy Honey: 12; NEWSCOM: 78 (Design Pics), 74 (Rick E. Martin), 70 (Cindy Yamanaka/Orange County Register/KRT); REX USA: 30, 40; ShutterStock, Inc.: 18 top (Douglas Freer), 65 (maga); The Baltimore Sun: 18 bottom (David Hobby), 47 (Jed Kirschbaum), 22, 44 (Jed Kirschbaum/Baltimore Examiner and Washington Examiner), 50 (Algerina Perna/Baltimore Examiner and Washington Examiner).

Library of Congress Cataloging-in-Publication Data

Jaye, Candace, 1955-
Life and death / Candace Jaye and John Malcolm.
p. cm. -- (On the record)
Includes bibliographical references and index.
ISBN-13: 978-0-531-22599-8 (pbk.)
ISBN-10: 0-531-22599-2
1. Juvenile delinquency--Maryland--Baltimore. I. Malcolm, John, 1963-
II. Title.
HV9106.B2J39 2012
362.74092--dc23

2011023760

Tod Olson, Series Editor
Marie O'Neill, Creative Director
Curriculum Concepts International, Production
Thanks to Candy J. Cooper and Sean McCollum

Life and Death

Some decisions are just that important.

Candace Jaye and John Malcolm

Contents

MOMENT OF TRUTH

How did one Wes Moore end up at a top
college and the other in prison?

Wes Moore was detained by the police for tagging in 1990. Moore, whose father had died suddenly eight years before, had been struggling with his grades and skipping school.

1
Busted

Wes Moore eyed the cans of spray paint in his friend Shea's backpack. "You wanna tag?" asked Shea.

It was a warm Saturday evening in October 1990. Wes turned to the wall of the Cue Lounge, a bar and billiards club in the Bronx in New York City. He sprayed his tag, *KK*, for Kid Kupid, and stood back to take a look. He had chosen his street name to advertise his charm with girls.

He was still admiring his work when he heard a police siren. Both boys took off, but Wes managed to run straight toward the police car. An officer forced him against the car, face down. He cuffed Wes and threw him into the backseat.

Wes couldn't believe it. He was being arrested. Then again, maybe it was the direction he'd been headed in for a while. Ever since his mother had moved Wes and his two sisters from southern Maryland to the Bronx, Wes hadn't been sure where he fit in. During the day he was one of the few black students at a private school that was mostly wealthy and white. His single mother worked multiple jobs to pay his tuition.

After school and on weekends, Wes hung out on the streets with kids like Shea, who ran drugs for a neighborhood dealer. In recent months, Wes's grades had dropped. He'd been caught skipping class and often didn't show up for school at all. He was on the verge of being expelled.

Soon Shea joined Wes in the patrol car, handcuffed but defiant. He swore at the cops. Wes told him to shut up.

One of the police officers climbed into the car and listened to the two boys argue. Before letting them go, the cop unloaded a lecture on them. "I see kids like you here every day," he said. "If you don't get smart, I am certain I will see you again."

The same year, in a development of row houses just outside of Baltimore, Maryland, another kid named Wes Moore got busted. It wasn't the cops who caught this Wes Moore, but his older brother, Tony.

Tony had often lectured Wes about avoiding the drug corners of Baltimore. "You're not built for this game," Tony would tell him. "You're smart, you can do other things."

But Wes cared more about what his brother *did* than what he said. Tony had been dealing drugs since before he was ten. By 18, he had people working for him. He wore the hustler's uniform, sporting everything from the fresh clothing to the gold chains around his neck. Wes was stuck with beat-up sneakers and old clothes. He wanted what his brother had.

One day Wes got a visit from Tony, who noticed a tower of shoe boxes in his younger brother's bedroom. Tony demanded to know where Wes had gotten the money to buy the shoes.

Wes claimed he had earned it by working parties as a DJ. Tony didn't believe him. When Wes insisted it was true, Tony punched his brother square in the face. Wes fell to the ground, and Tony pinned his arms down and kept swinging at him. One blow after another found a target until their mother, Mary Moore, burst in and stopped the beating.

The next day, Mary Moore discovered Wes's stash of pills, marijuana, and cocaine in shoe boxes under his bed. She flushed $4,000 worth of drugs down the toilet. She ordered Wes to stop selling drugs and said she'd keep checking his room for them. His drug dealing was putting the whole family in danger, she said.

Wes Moore had been caught. The next move was his.

Wes Moore from the Bronx became a star student and ended up at Oxford University in Great Britain (top). The other Wes Moore was sentenced to life in prison at Jessup Correctional Institution in Maryland (bottom).

2
Seeing Double

Ten years after Wes Moore got stopped by the Bronx police, he picked up a copy of the *Baltimore Sun*. "Hopkins Senior a Rhodes Scholar," read the newspaper headline. The story was about Moore himself. The one-time graffiti vandal had just won one of the world's most prestigious scholarships.

Moore had traveled a long way from the backseat of the Bronx patrol car. He had studied at Johns Hopkins University and in South Africa. He had worked for the mayor of Baltimore. Now he was on his way to Oxford University in England.

But around that same time, there was another article in the *Sun* that Moore couldn't get out of his mind. "Two Wanted in Officer's Killing Are Captured in Philadelphia," the paper had announced on February 20, 2000. The two suspects had allegedly shot a police officer during a jewelry store robbery in Baltimore County. The suspects were brothers. And the younger one's name was Wes Moore.

Moore was rattled. Not only did the two men share a name, they had been born in Maryland, just a few years apart. Both Moores had grown up without a father, done poorly in school as kids, and had trouble with police.

A couple of months before Moore left for Oxford, his namesake was sentenced to life in prison without parole.

Four years later, Moore finished his degree at Oxford and took a job as an investment banker. But he was still obsessed with the other Wes Moore. How had they ended up on such different paths? Entire lives seemed to hang on small decisions, made early on when you didn't know they mattered. The outcome could be triumph or disaster, Oxford or jail.

Moore finally sat down and wrote a letter to the other Wes Moore at Jessup Correctional Institution in central Maryland. "Dear Wes: Please allow me to introduce myself . . . " He went on to ask a few questions: Did Wes see his brother, Tony, who was also serving a life sentence at

A cell in a maximum-security prison in Maryland. Wes Moore from Baltimore was sentenced to life without parole in 2001. He will spend the rest of his life in a prison like this one.

Jessup? What happened to lead to the robbery and the murder? How did Moore's life end up where it did? Wes Moore the banker sent the letter, not expecting to hear back.

A month later he received a reply. Two letters turned into dozens. Questions were asked and stories exchanged. And for the Wes Moore who wrote the first letter, a shot in the dark turned into an all-consuming project. He decided he would uncover the details of the other Moore's life and reflect on the shape of his own. He would tell the story of two lives that could have been different. "The chilling truth," he would write, "is that his story could have been mine. The tragedy is that my story could have been his."

Young kids play baseball in an abandoned lot in the South Bronx. The neighborhood was plagued by drugs and violence during the years when Wes Moore the author lived in a neighborhood to the north.

3
Decisions

Wesley John Moore was born in West Baltimore in 1974. That was less than 26 years before he would be sent to prison for life.

His mother was the first in her family to go to college. While raising Wes, she earned a two-year degree and was accepted to Johns Hopkins University. But then the government cut back on education funding, and she had no choice but to drop out and find work. She got a full-time job as a medical secretary.

At $6.50 an hour, Mary Moore could barely afford her children's food and clothing. There was no money left over for child care, and Wes's father wasn't around to help. By the age of six, Wes was on his own much of the time.

Wes's half brother, Tony, didn't live with Wes and his mother, but Wes saw Tony often and looked to him for guidance. Tony taught his little brother the harsh survival code of the West Baltimore streets. If people disrespect you, Tony told Wes, respond so fiercely that they'll never dare to do it again.

Wes followed his big brother's example. He was arrested at age eight for pulling a knife on a boy during a fight. He failed classes at school and had to repeat sixth grade. He spent his time on the street, hanging out with other troubled kids.

Mary Moore's response was to get Wes away from West Baltimore. When Wes was 12, they moved to Baltimore County, just outside the city. They found a house in the leafy Dundee Village housing complex.

But Wes gravitated to what he knew. One Saturday afternoon, he spotted a boy standing on a street corner wearing a cool-looking headset and a sparkling gold ring. Wes asked the boy where he could get a headset of his own, and soon he was wearing one, working as a lookout for a local drug dealer. It was Wes's job to keep an eye out for the police and call the drug dealer when he spotted them.

This new life brought Wes power and status. He moved on from his job as a lookout and started dealing drugs himself. With the profits he bought new clothes, jewelry, and the shoes that earned him a beating from his brother in 1990.

That beating, along with the warning he got from his mother, could have served as a wake-up call for young Wes. But when his mother flushed his drugs down the toilet, Wes flew into a rage. Then he started storing his drugs at his girlfriend's apartment.

The following year, a fight over someone else's girlfriend got Wes into his first serious trouble with the law. He was showing the girl out of his house at 1 A.M. when her jealous boyfriend—a guy named Ray—jumped Wes and beat him up.

When the girl finally pulled Ray off, Wes didn't hesitate. He ducked into the house, pulled out a handgun, and tore into the street to chase Ray down. A friend joined him, and they ran through the streets firing shots at Ray. A bullet found its mark, and Ray fell wounded behind a car.

Wes ran home and burst into the house. He ran past his mother to hide his gun and clean himself up. He had barely finished when the police arrived. He would spend the next six months in juvenile hall for attempted murder.

While he was locked up, another girlfriend, Alicia, gave birth to a baby boy. At 16, Wes was both a father and a convicted criminal.

Students march in formation at Valley Forge Military Academy and College in Pennsylvania. Wes Moore from the Bronx was sent to Valley Forge by his mother when he was 12.

4
A Bold Move

In 1991, while Wes did time in juvenile hall in Baltimore, Wes Moore the future Rhodes scholar was driving his mother crazy in the Bronx. After getting caught by the police, he had gone right back to tagging. Administrators at his private school warned his mother that he was about to be expelled. *I lost my husband*, Joy Moore said to herself, *I'm not going to lose my son.*

Wes's father had been a popular journalist for a Washington, D.C., radio station.

One evening when Wes was three, his father collapsed and died at their home in a Maryland suburb. A rare virus had made his throat swell shut.

After her husband's death, Wes's mother felt overwhelmed. She worried about their neighborhood, where crime was on the rise. One day, in desperation, she called her parents in the Bronx: "I need help."

Wes moved with his mother and two sisters to the Bronx. His grandparents had even stricter rules than his mother. But Wes found a way around them. By the age of 12, his grades had slipped. He skipped school to hang out on the streets. He was put on academic probation.

Joy Moore knew she had to do something. With financial help from her parents, she sent Wes to Valley Forge Military Academy in rural Wayne, Pennsylvania.

Once again Wes found himself dropped into an alien world. He hated everything about Valley Forge, from the school grounds to the people to the military commands: "right face," and "left face," and "parade rest." How could his mother do this to him? In his first four days at the school, Wes ran away five times.

On his fifth attempt, he was caught and dragged back to school. His colonel offered him one five-minute phone call to get his head straight. Wes dialed his mother and pleaded to go home.

Joy Moore refused. "It's time to stop running," she told him.

The mural on the side of this building is a memorial
to young men killed by street violence in Baltimore.
The initials, LB, stand for "Lost Boys."

5
Last Chance

Back in Baltimore, Wesley John Moore had just finished his six-month sentence in juvenile hall. He enrolled at Lake Clifton High School. Lake Clifton was one of the largest and poorest-performing public high schools in the country. Some people referred to it as a "dropout factory." When Wes cut class, no one dragged him back or called his mother. In the middle of his first year at Lake Clifton, Wes dropped out.

Wes's education had been cut short, but his family grew. He had a second child with Alicia and two more with another woman, Cheryl, who lived nearby. By 1996 he had two girlfriends and four children looking to him for support. He had no diploma or job skills. With his criminal record, Wes was nearly unemployable—except in the one area he knew well.

Wes had become a leader in the drug trade. He ran his own crew like a business, sometimes making more than $4,000 in a day.

By his early twenties, Wes understood that he had to make a change. He had been shot at and had attended the funerals of friends. He had been busted and jailed many times. Cheryl, the mother of two of his children, was a heroin addict.

A friend told Wes about Job Corps, a federal program designed to help disadvantaged youths find work. Two weeks later Wes was on a Job Corps campus outside of Baltimore. For seven months he trained as a carpenter. He built a five-foot-tall house for his daughter. It was the most successful project in the class. He also earned a high school degree by passing the General Educational Development (GED) test. He was reading, it turned out, at a college level.

Wes graduated from Job Corps with a diploma and a skill. But finding steady work wasn't easy. He worked as a landscaper and a carpenter, but both jobs were temporary. He found a job preparing meals at a restaurant in a mall. He worked ten-hour days but had little to show for it.

A 24-year-old member of the Job Corps learns to do electrical wiring. Job Corps provides free education and job training to qualifying young people ages 16 and up.

The pressures that weighed Wes down before Job Corps hadn't gone away. Alicia, Cheryl, and his mother all needed money. He managed for a year before he grew too frustrated.

One day when Wes finished chopping vegetables at his restaurant job, he decided to visit his old West Baltimore neighborhood. The place felt familiar. Little had changed. It would be easy enough, Wes thought, to bring home a package of cocaine, cook it up, and turn it into crack for sale on the street.

A cadet does push-ups at Valley Forge Military Academy. The academy's mission is to foster "character development, personal motivation, physical development, and leadership" in its students.

6
The Turnaround

In Wayne, Pennsylvania, Wes Moore realized he was stuck at Valley Forge Military Academy. So the new cadet started to accept his fate.

The school was modeled after the U.S. military. Cadets were organized into companies of 100 students each. They could move up in rank if they did well in class and mastered the strict routine of military life. Blaring music woke them at dawn. Every day they polished their black leather shoes with their own spit.

As Wes suffered through the rigid schedule, he began to bond with the other cadets. He also found a mentor in a 19-year-old captain named Ty Hill. Wes's mother knew her son needed a male role model in his life, and she had asked Hill to watch over him. "I can try to teach you how to be a good human being," she had often told Wes, "but I can never teach you how to be a man."

Wes was drawn to Hill, who led the most impressive company of cadets at Valley Forge. Hill commanded respect by example, not by scare tactics. Hill embodied a new version of manhood for Wes—one more impressive than the bullying he'd seen pass for manhood back in the Bronx.

Wes also responded to the clear system of rewards at Valley Forge. If he got good grades, he earned the right to leave the campus. If he polished his shoes to a high shine, he was rewarded with a later "lights out" at night.

Showing leadership brought added benefits, and it turned out that Wes could lead. A star basketball player, he was the youngest starter on the high school varsity team. He became president of his senior class and climbed in military rank.

In 1998, while the other Wes struggled to stay out of the Baltimore drug trade, Wes Moore graduated as the highest-ranking student out of 750 cadets.

This photo shows the visiting area at a maximum-security prison in Maryland. At Jessup Correctional, Moore occasionally gets visits from his family, but he finds it painful to say good-bye when their time is up.

7
Two Wes Moores

In 2005, after graduating from high school, Johns Hopkins, and Oxford, Wes Moore stood in a large visitor's room at Jessup prison in Maryland. Armed guards paced the floor. Long tables with low metal dividers separated the imprisoned from the free. The prisoners were marched in, and there he spotted the other Wes Moore.

The details of the crime that had put Wesley John Moore in jail were well known in the Baltimore area. On February 7, 2000, four masked men waving guns ran into a jewelry store in Pikesville, Maryland. They smashed the glass cases, grabbed $438,000 worth of watches and jewelry, and fled out the door.

Sergeant Bruce Prothero, a Baltimore police officer who worked security at the store, ran after the gunmen with his weapon drawn. As he searched the parking lot for the robbers, he ducked behind a car for protection. By some terrible stroke of fortune, he had hidden next to one of the getaway cars. A gloved hand, clutching a handgun, reached out of the window. Three shots struck Prothero at point-blank range. The cars screeched off, leaving Prothero, a father of five young children, to die on the street.

Police march at Sergeant Bruce Prothero's funeral. "It seems like forever since I saw him. But the event itself seems like yesterday," said his widow, Ann Prothero, three months after the murder.

Within two weeks, all four robbers had been arrested. Tony Moore escaped the death penalty by confessing to shooting Prothero. Wes Moore insisted on a trial. He claimed he hadn't been involved in the robbery. But DNA evidence placed him at the scene of the crime, and he was convicted of murder and sentenced to life in prison.

Four years later, Wes Moore the prisoner sat down across from Wes Moore the investment banker. The prisoner wore a long goatee and a knit cap, reflecting his conversion to Islam in jail. The men shook hands and began the first of dozens of conversations, many of which seemed to lead to the same question: why did one Wes Moore end up in prison and the other at Oxford?

One day Wes Moore the prisoner came up with an answer. "We will do what others expect of us," he said. "If they expect us to graduate, we will graduate. If they expect us to get a job, we will get a job. If they expect us to go to jail, then that's where we will end up, too."

Across the table, Wes Moore the banker wasn't so sure. At some point, you have to take control of your own life, he thought. But he agreed that the expectations of the people around you are important. As he wrote later: "Other people hold on to your hopes and dreams for you until you're ready to take them on yourself." His mother had held onto his dreams until he was ready to live them.

The two men often talked about the book that Moore would write, *The Other Wes*

Wes Moore the author walks down the Baltimore street where Wes Moore the prisoner grew up. Beside him is his mother, Joy Moore, "the rock of our family," he says.

Moore: One Name, Two Fates. They didn't know then that it would become a best seller and that Moore would tour the country to promote it.

On his tours, everyone would ask him: what matters most? Education, he'd tell them. As Moore's grandfather often said, "Education is like a skeleton key. If you can get that skeleton key, it can open any door."

People also ask whether the other Wes Moore supported the idea of the book. Moore the author repeats what the prisoner has told him: "I have wasted every opportunity that I've ever had in life, and I'm going to die in here. If you can do something to help people understand . . . then I think you should do it."

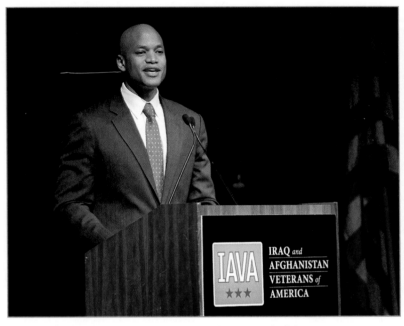

Wes Moore speaks at an event for Iraq and Afghanistan Veterans of America. "So little separates us from another life altogether," he says.

Wes Moore

Born:

October 15, 1978

Grew up:

Takoma Park, Maryland, and the Bronx

Education:

Valley Forge Military Academy and College,
Johns Hopkins University, Oxford University

Military service:

Paratrooper and captain in the U.S. Army;
served in Afghanistan, 2005–2006

Life's work:

Author, businessman, advocate for veterans, and
mentor for youths

Website:

theotherwesmoore.com

Author of:

The Other Wes Moore: One Name, Two Fates

He says:

"When we're young, it sometimes seems as if the
world doesn't exist outside our city, our block,
our house, our room. We make decisions based
on what we see in that limited world. What
changed was that I found myself surrounded by
people . . . who kept pushing me to see . . . the
boundless possibilities of the wider world . . . "

BIRD IN A CAGE

Maria Reyes was raised on gang violence. By
the age of 13, she had already been arrested for
carjacking, drugs, and weapons possession.
She wanted out—but she'd have to risk
her life to make it happen.

Maria Reyes was born in East Los Angeles. When she was just 11 years old, she joined the same gang that her father and grandfather had belonged to.

8

Witness

The court officer stepped into the lobby and called her name. *Here we go,* Maria thought. She followed the officer inside and walked the lonely center aisle to the witness stand.

The previous spring, Maria had been jumped by several members of a rival gang. She and her best homeboy, Paco, had tracked them down, and Paco had shot one of them. It was payback, the oldest rule of gang life.

A member of the rival gang had been arrested for the murder, and now he was on trial. Maria and Paco had been subpoenaed as witnesses, and they both planned to testify that the innocent defendant had been the shooter.

When Maria was seated in the witness stand, she looked around the courtroom. One side was filled with her homies, the members of her gang. They had pledged their lives to protect each other. The members of the rival gang, who sat on the other side of the courtroom, had made the same pledge to their fellow members.

As Maria scanned the courtroom, she made eye contact with an African American woman. The woman had tears on her face and a young daughter on her lap. Could she be—?

Maria was in court to testify that an innocent guy was guilty of murder, and here was his mother. Maria tried to push the image from her head. She had a job to do. She was there to fulfill the code of her family and the gang—protect your own. But she couldn't help seeing her own mother in the woman's sad face, and herself as the little girl.

Protect your own. It was that simple.

Maria looked over at Paco. She noticed he didn't look nervous at all. He was completely positive that she would lie to protect him—even if it meant sending an innocent man to prison. Her whole gang expected her to identify the rival gang member as the shooter.

She could hear her father's advice ringing in her head. He had grown up in the gang and remained loyal, even in prison. He had already told her she needed to lie for Paco.

But recently Maria had felt her loyalty shaken. New ideas were taking root, planted by new friendships at school and the books her English teacher kept assigning. Maria had begun asking herself questions: *Does it have to be this way—hating and fighting and shooting and dying? Could there be something better? Could I choose something better?*

But if she told the truth, she knew she might pay a terrible price. If she named Paco as the murderer, her own gang would probably turn on her. They might even kill her.

Maria tried to act cool as the lawyers began laying down questions. "Why did those guys attack you? Where were you on the night

of the shooting? Who were you with?"
Maria answered each one. Her gaze shifted
between the two sides of the courtroom.

The questions pushed Maria toward
the point of no return. Should she
uphold the code of the gang? Or should
she speak the truth and deal with the
consequences?

Lives—including her own—hung in the
balance.

Teenagers hang out in an urban playground. "Throughout my life, I've always heard the same thing: 'You can't go against your own people,'" Maria says.

9
Jumped In

For Maria, joining the gang was never really a choice. Gang life was part of her world, from her earliest memories on. She had been born in East Los Angeles, a tough neighborhood with a deep history of poverty and crime. East L.A. was a gritty, ragged place. Swirls of gang graffiti layered bridges and walls. Steel bars and metal gates sealed off houses and shops from break-ins. Broken beer bottles sparkled in the gutters, and weeds overran empty lots.

But Maria didn't know anything different. East L.A. was home.

Her dad and grandfather were *veteranos*—veterans in their Latino gang. Her dad had once dreamed of being a boxer, but most dreams died in East L.A. Her mother was a great cook and a hard worker, but she never got past second grade.

For her fifth birthday, Maria had hoped for a mountain bike. Instead she opened a box to find a pair of shiny red boxing gloves and a note from her dad: "Life is tough. When it knocks you down, I want you to get up swinging." Maria took his words to heart.

Shortly after that birthday, her family visited her grandparents' house. Her mother tried to catch Maria to braid her hair, maybe even put a dress on the little

Maria's father gave her a pair of boxing gloves for her fifth birthday so she could learn to protect herself.

tomboy. Maria escaped by climbing the tree in the front yard, out of her mom's reach.

She was still hiding in the tree when she heard sirens closing in. Her older cousin was coming up the street. She liked him a lot. He was tall and strong and told her bedtime stories. As he approached the house, Maria heard five shots. Her cousin fell to the concrete, shot by police for reasons that never became clear. He died shortly after, another victim of gang life in East L.A.

Maria was still in grade school when the violence hit even closer to home. Her father was arrested for a gang-related crime he didn't commit. The judge sentenced him to ten years in a maximum-security prison.

Overnight, Maria's mother was left alone to raise three young kids. She worked three jobs, day and night. She cleaned the homes of rich people, scrubbed toilets at big hotels, and sewed fancy clothes in sweat-shop factories. Even so, she struggled to pay the bills and keep food on the table. "We don't have the luxury of crying," Maria remembered her grandfather saying. "Because for people like us, if we started, we'd be crying for a lifetime."

Maria wasn't much for crying, anyway. Whatever sadness or despair she felt quickly turned to anger. She would fight with anyone, no matter the punishment. In fourth grade, she was expelled from a school for punching a teacher.

Maria was short, but by age 11 she had proven she was plenty tough. She was sitting on the porch one summer evening when a member of her father's gang walked up. "Do it now?" he asked her.

Maria nodded. She wasn't scared. She didn't even feel excited. Joining the gang was just the next step in growing up, and it was time to get it done. She was about to get "jumped in"—endure a major beating to earn her place in the gang.

Gang members gathered in an alley across the street from Maria's house. For the first round, a group of older girls circled around her. Maria knew she wasn't supposed to fight back. That was the custom. But when someone slugged her in the nose, her instincts kicked in. She threw a punch.

She had broken the rules. The leader added extra time to the first-round beating.

For round two, gang members formed two facing lines—ten *cholos* on the right, ten *chicas* on the left. Maria's mission was to pass between them. This time she could return the punches and kicks. But she had to be standing at the end.

She strode into the human tunnel. She ducked and battled while taking blow after blow. She fell near the end and someone stomped on her leg. She fought her way to her feet and stumbled to the finish.

To Maria, the ten-minute ordeal felt like it had taken two hours. Her nose was broken. One of her eyes was swelling shut. At the hospital, doctors found she had a broken arm and leg. But the pain was worth it—she was now a warrior like her dad. She belonged to the gang, and the gang belonged to her.

A 16-year-old girl looks out through the fence at a juvenile hall in California. In 2007 more than 17,500 young people were locked up in California.

10
The Cage

In 1992 Maria and her family moved from East L.A. to Long Beach, a city 20 miles south of downtown Los Angeles. Its neighborhoods are a patchwork of white, Latino, black, and Asian communities.

Maria brought her gang connections with her. She was only 12, but she was already a "working soldier"—an active member in the gang. She wore the belt buckle and the colors, with the bandanna dangling from the back pocket of her jeans.

Maria refused to hang back like many of the older girls in the gang. She belonged to a new generation of *chicas* who were determined to act as tough as the guys. She fell right into step dealing drugs, selling guns, and fending off challenges from rival gangs.

Before her one-year anniversary in the gang, Maria had already been arrested and locked up. The police caught her in a stolen car. They found drugs in the trunk and in her pockets. The driver of the car had slipped away, and Maria refused to name him. The result was her first stint in a juvenile detention center, or "juvie," as everyone called it. To Maria, getting locked up in the detention center seemed like just another step in growing up.

Maria was one of the youngest girls in the center, but she knew how to protect herself. When older girls tested her, she fought back. It was the only way to make them respect her, she figured.

During what should have been her middle school years, Maria spent more time in juvie than she did in school. She was busted seven times before the age of 14. Cops would see her on the street in gang colors and stop her for questioning. Once she was locked up for carrying a gun. Usually she was busted for violating the terms of her probation.

After one arrest she chose to go to a boot camp program instead of juvie. The boot camp guards enforced military-style discipline—5 A.M. wake-ups, cold showers, push-ups, and laps around the track. The guards barked orders like drill sergeants. "You may be something on the street, but you're nothing in here!" they shouted in

Female offenders march at a California boot camp.
Boot camps are very strict programs run by drill
instructors. Maria dropped out of one during her
middle school years.

her face. Maria couldn't stand it. She left the program and was bused back to juvie.

The early 1990s were an especially harsh time to be a kid in the poor neighborhoods of L.A. and Long Beach. To a lot of people living there, it seemed like a war zone. Latino gangs, black gangs, and Asian gangs battled for control of the streets. They trapped entire neighborhoods in an ongoing cycle of attacks and revenge. Drive-by shootings were daily events.

Gang life was dragging Maria down, but she felt she couldn't leave. It seemed that the only thing she could do was embrace the violence. No one made it out of her neighborhood anyway. She figured she'd be pregnant by 15, like her mom. Or locked up like her dad. Or dead like her cousin and other gang members she'd run with. She had already attended more funerals in her life than birthday parties.

At 14, Maria was arrested for fighting, skipping school, and missing appointments with her parole officer. All three offenses violated her probation. She served another couple of months in juvie and then joined a line of teen gang members in front of a judge. She was dressed in a blue jumpsuit with "Property of Juvenile Hall" stenciled on the back. Her wrists and ankles were cuffed.

The judge stared down at her. "It's clear you haven't learned anything, and I don't know what else to do with you," he said. "You have violated parole time after time. It seems clear you're on your way to becoming a career criminal. If you're ever in my courtroom again, you'll be behind bars until you're 18."

Maria glared back. *Who is this guy kidding?* she thought. *The game is rigged. I'll mess up or the cops will cook up some bogus charge and I'll be right back here. It's just a matter of time.* She thought about giving the judge the finger, but the cuffs made it impossible to lift her hands.

Maria was beyond caring, but her parole officer stood up for her. He got her sentenced to house arrest. Maria would be able to leave home only to go to school. The officer also got her enrolled at Woodrow Wilson High, a school across town. He hoped it would be far enough from her neighborhood to help her stay out of trouble.

Maria was sent to Room 203 of Woodrow Wilson High School. If she got in trouble there, a judge threatened, she'd be locked up until she turned 18.

Maria was already on edge when she entered Room 203 of Wilson High. Her face was marred by a black eye from a recent fight. Still, the staff had insisted on taking her ID picture—the photo that would appear in the yearbook. She was wearing an ankle monitor so her parole officer could keep track of her movements. And she didn't know a single person at the school.

I might as well wear a prison jumpsuit with "Jump Me" taped on the back, she thought.

She dropped her backpack and took a seat in the back of the room.

She scanned the rest of her ninth-grade remedial English class. It was a mix of blacks, Asians, Latinos, and one white boy who looked terrified. Most of them took buses from the poorer neighborhoods of Long Beach. Several classmates gave Maria suspicious looks, and she glared right back.

But Maria also noticed the defeat in everyone's eyes. They were all no-hopers, kids everybody knew were on the fast track to dropping out. Through the years they had all gotten the message from teachers and classmates—you're lazy, you're dumb, you're doomed. The teachers seemed to *want* them to quit school so they could focus on the "good" students.

The teacher had scribbled "Erin Gruwell" on the chalkboard. She was really young, really white, and faced the class with a goofy smile on her face. She wore a polka dot dress and a pearl necklace and had chalk dust on her butt. *This lady ain't going to last a week*, Maria thought. That was one truth she knew all her classmates could agree on.

Maria had a lot of reasons for hating school. Teachers seemed to get a kick out of making her feel stupid. She remembered her shame when grade school teachers had made fun of her "Spanglish"—the mix of broken English and Spanish she had grown up speaking. And she had only fallen further and further behind while stuck in the revolving doors of juvenile hall. She was sick of people saying they wanted to help and then turning on her when she disappointed them. *As soon as you catch me messing up, or see what a lousy student I am, you'll bail, too, Erin Gruwell,* Maria thought.

Maria skipped school sometimes, but most days she made the long bus ride to and from Wilson High. When she wasn't in school, her probation required her to be at home.

None of her homies pressured her to run with the gang during this time. When Maria said she didn't want to do something, it was begging for trouble to ask twice.

One day in school, Ms. Gruwell laid down a line of tape on the floor. "We're going to play a game, the Line Game," she announced in her cheery voice. "I'm going to ask a question, and if it applies to you, I want you to stand on the line." She asked a couple easy questions, like "How many of you have the

new Snoop Dogg album?" Almost everybody put their toes on the line.

Then the questions got more serious.

"How many of you have been shot at?"
Most people touched the line. Then they
stepped back for the next question.

"How many of you have a friend or rela-
tive who was or is in juvenile hall or jail?"
Maria stepped forward. Many of the other
kids put their feet on the line, too.

"How many of you have lost a friend to
gang violence?" Almost all of the class
stepped on the line. "Two friends?" A few
students stepped back. "Three?"

Maria kept her face still as the class played
Ms. G's "game." But it struck her as she
glanced at the other students: *We're all different colors and come from different gangs*

and neighborhoods. But we're all dealing with the same stuff. We feel the same pain. They were like soldiers who had all survived combat. She felt a strange bond with the rest of them.

When it came time to write in her journal, Maria didn't hold back. It was another assignment Ms. G had given the class—to write every day about their experiences, thoughts, and feelings. "Write the truth," she had said.

Want the truth? Maria thought. *Okay, here it is.* "I hate Erin Gruwell. I hate Erin Gruwell," Maria wrote. "If I wasn't on probation, I'd probably shank her."

Maria handed in her journal. She was sure Ms. G would finally call her probation officer. Then it would be a quick trip back to juvie and Maria's lousy life would be back on its lousy track.

But nothing happened. When Maria got her journal back she flipped to what she had written. The only comment Ms. G had made was a big smiley face in red pen. Maria looked at it in disbelief. *What is with this woman?* she wondered.

It was that April that Maria got jumped by the rival gang. A few weeks later, she was in the car with her friend Paco when he spotted the gang's leader. Paco got out of the car and, as Maria watched, gunned the guy down. Then Paco turned to Maria and said, "This is for you."

Another man was arrested and charged with the murder. Maria was an eyewitness. She would be subpoenaed to testify at the trial about what she had seen that day.

This is a page from the diary that Anne Frank wrote while she was in hiding from the Nazis. To her surprise, Maria found herself inspired by Anne's story.

12
The Door Opens

Maria returned to Room 203 for her sophomore year. She was annoyed that Ms. Gruwell was back again. But she noticed that other kids in class were warming up to their peppy English teacher. Unlike most teachers, Ms. G seemed willing to listen just as much as she talked. Maria still thought she was a fake, but she had to admit that Ms. G was no quitter.

Ms. Gruwell told the class that the theme for the school year was tolerance. She handed out the first book. It was *The Diary of a Young Girl*, by Anne Frank—a true story about a Jewish girl and her family who were forced to hide from the Nazis during World War II.

Maria frowned at the girl's picture on the cover. *Another book about some white kid*, she thought. "Why have I got to read this?" she asked Ms. Gruwell.

"I think you're going to find yourself in the pages of this book," Ms. G replied. Maria laughed in her face.

Maria was still under house arrest. Her mom hadn't been able to pay the electric bill, so there was no TV. Maria had nothing better to do, so she went ahead and started reading. She wanted to prove to Ms. G just how wrong she was. *Find myself in a book? Get real*, Maria thought. *They don't write books about bad girls like me.*

But Maria got caught up in the story. Anne Frank had guts and a sense of humor. Maria wondered how Anne's romance with a boy in the hiding place would turn out. And when the Nazis started closing in on Anne, Maria was rooting for her. Maria even found herself talking about the book with Ms. Gruwell.

Then Maria read a passage that hit her like a ton of bricks. While Anne wanders through the family's secret hideout, she feels trapped within its walls like a bird in a cage. She longs to be able to fly away.

The words stunned Maria. That was how *she* felt, trapped in her violent, luckless life. But she'd never had the words to express it.

When she finished the book, Maria held it in her arms and cried. She felt knocked off balance, like someone had tilted her world.

The next day Maria threw the book at Ms. Gruwell. "Why didn't you tell me?"

"Tell you what?" asked the startled teacher.

"Why didn't you tell me Anne Frank didn't make it? She died." Maria was in despair. If a nice girl like Anne couldn't make it, she asked Ms. Gruwell, what hope was there for someone like *her?*

Ms. G stammered, trying to come up with a response. Then a classmate, Darius, spoke up. "She did make it, Maria," he said. "She's going to go on living even after she died because she wrote. How many of our friends have died and they didn't even get an obituary?"

The idea landed hard on Maria. Her dead friends from the gang were gone with hardly anyone to remember them. But one brave girl who shared her story of fear and hope would never be forgotten.

In the weeks that followed, Maria's class studied more about the Holocaust—the systematic murder of millions of Jews by the Nazis. They took a field trip to the Museum of Tolerance in L.A. They sat down to dinner with Holocaust survivors to hear their stories firsthand.

Maria felt something changing in her heart and mind. Here she was, reading about and meeting people who had suffered from the most terrible hatred and violence. Yet even as they faced terror and death, they refused to give up hope for a better world. If they still felt that way after all they had been through, why couldn't Maria?

Back in the *barrio*, Maria's gang-mates noticed the changes in her. "I feel you slipping away, a little each day," Paco said. "And at times I have a hard time recognizing you."

Maria tried to explain. New thoughts and feelings were pulling her in a different direction. She felt alone and confused, caught between worlds. But her longtime homies didn't get it. It was like she was speaking a language they didn't understand.

Meanwhile, the trial for the murder of the rival gang member was approaching. Maria knew everyone expected her to protect Paco in court by identifying the innocent defendant as the shooter.

Maria visited her dad in prison a few days before the trial. She loved and trusted him deeply. He told her it was her duty to the gang to lie for Paco's sake. Telling the truth would dishonor the family and put her in danger.

But Maria's soft-spoken mother surprised her. Before Maria left for court, her mother asked her what she was going to say on the witness stand. "I'm going to protect my own . . . you know how it is," Maria answered.

"I know how it is, but why does it always have to be that way?" her mom replied.

In her whole life, Maria couldn't remember her mom ever questioning the gang code. The family had always obeyed it, even though it landed Maria in juvie and her dad in prison. It was the law of the hood, of life.

Why does it always have to be that way? The question echoed in Maria's mind.

Erin Gruwell's students at Woodrow Wilson High School called themselves the "Freedom Writers." All 150 of Gruwell's Freedom Writers graduated from high school, and many went on to college.

In the courtroom, all eyes were on the witness stand. The lawyer finally asked the question Maria had been waiting for: "Who shot the guy?"

Maria felt a kind of peace settle on her. Her thoughts were clear. Doing things the same old way never changed anything. Paco had pulled the trigger this time. Next time, they'd hunt down Paco and shoot him. It would never stop.

Meanwhile, brave people like Anne Frank had looked into the ugly face of hatred and had still been able to feel hope. It was suddenly obvious what Maria had to do.

"Paco did it," she answered. "Paco shot the guy."

The courtroom froze for what seemed like hours. Then the world began to move again. As he was led out of the courtroom, Paco glared at Maria. "Of all people, you're the last person I thought would betray me," he said.

Maria returned home and went back to school. She felt bad about sending Paco to prison and trashing the loyalty she had promised the gang. She knew she had destroyed her ties with them. That usually meant a trip to the hospital—or the cemetery.

Her father was furious when he found out what Maria had done. "You're no daughter of mine," he told her on the phone. "You have brought shame to the family." But deep down, Maria knew she'd made the right choice.

Paco was sentenced to 25 years in prison, and Maria received multiple threats afterward. But nothing happened. No one drove by and blasted her as she got off the bus after school. No one knifed her on the way to the store. It seemed like the word had been passed—*keep your hands off Maria*. Her family's reputation must be protecting her, she figured.

Maria felt like she'd started a race toward a distant finish line, a race she was not sure she would finish. But she was running *her* race. She wasn't just sprinting wherever gang life told her to run. Ms. G was always telling the class that education was the best way out—the way out of being poor, powerless, and in prison. Maria was starting to believe her. She felt a new kind of strength growing inside her.

Two years later, Maria stood in line, listening for her name to be called. For some reason, it reminded her of waiting in line at juvie to see the judge. She wished the judge could see her now, graduating from Wilson High. She was the first in her family to complete high school. In a couple of months, she would be the first to go to college.

Maria heard her name called and walked across the stage in the bright sunlight. Beyond the fence, she heard her family members whooping. She glanced into the audience and spotted her mom and dad. Her dad had gotten out of prison and quit the gang. He and Maria had made their peace.

The graduation gown Maria wore felt like wings.

Maria's father went on to earn his General Educational Development certificate. Today he works in a gang prevention program.

Maria and other students in Ms. Gruwell's English class published their writings in a book called *The Freedom Writers Diary*. Money from sales of the book was used to create the Freedom Writers Foundation and help pay for college for the students from Room 203. Their story was later told in the movie *Freedom Writers*.

Maria Reyes graduated from California State University–Long Beach and is planning a career in education. She travels to schools across the U.S. to share her story with students and teachers.

Maria Reyes was the first person in her family to graduate from high school. She is now a college graduate and works for the Freedom Writers Foundation.

Maria Reyes

Born:

May 5, 1980

Grew up:

East Los Angeles and Long Beach, California

Life's work:

To advocate for people who others have written off

Day job:

Speaks to youths, educators, and community leaders
on behalf of the Freedom Writers Foundation

Contributor to:

*The Freedom Writers Diary: How a Teacher and 150
Teens Used Writing to Change Themselves and the
World Around Them*

First book she connected to:

The Diary of a Young Girl, Anne Frank

Other favorite books:

The Count of Monte Cristo, Alexander Dumas
A New Earth, Eckhart Tolle
One Hundred Years of Solitude, Gabriel García Márquez
White Oleander, Janet Fitch

Favorite quote:

"Intelligence plus character—that is the goal of
true education."
—Martin Luther King Jr.

A Conversation with Author
Candace Jaye

Q *What was your process for researching and writing the Wes Moore profile?*

A I read Moore's book, *The Other Wes Moore*, as well as newspaper and magazine stories about both Wes Moores. I also interviewed Wes Moore the author. As for deciding what to write: like Moore, I looked for the key decision points in each man's life and highlighted them.

Q *What did you find to be the most interesting similarity between the two Wes Moores?*

A They both grew up in the 1980s, during a destructive crack cocaine epidemic. Early on, that drug culture defined manhood for both boys, especially since they both grew up without fathers.

Q *How did the differences in their environments as kids affect the trajectory of their lives?*

A Wes Moore the author's parents and grand-parents earned college degrees and became professionals. His destiny was rooted in their example.

That is in contrast to the other Wes Moore, whose mother was forced to cut her college career short. Without a network of successful relatives or a success story of her own, Mary Moore was unable to instill high expectations in her son. That left the eye-for-an-eye influence of Wes's older brother, who was a drug dealer.

Q *What do you take away from this story?*

A External support from a family, a school, and a larger community is essential. Education is absolutely essential. And then there's the matter of personal character. It's as if nothing great can be achieved without a person's strong, sustained conviction—and resilience. I think of a plastic Bozo the Clown punching bag that a three-year-old knocks down only to have it spring right back up. You try to achieve, life takes its whacks, and you have to spring back up every time.

A Conversation with Author
John Malcolm

Q *What was your process for researching and writing the profile of Maria Reyes?*

A Maria took the time to do a two-hour phone interview with me. I asked her a lot of questions about how she had felt, what she'd heard, and other details. She was kind and patient, even when I called back with dozens of follow-up questions. I also had the pleasure of watching a video of her doing a school presentation. She's great in front of an audience!

Q *What struck you most about Maria's story?*

A You don't often meet people who open themselves to new experiences and allow those experiences to inspire them to improve their lives. But Maria saw a dead end waiting for her, and she found the courage to say, "I want something with hope." She then did the very, very hard and gutsy work to remake her identity and her life.

Q *Why was Maria able to make it out when a lot of others never do?*

A It seems her mother gave her an opening by suggesting that Maria's life could be better. And Maria eventually rallied to the support and inspiration of her classmates and a special teacher, Erin Gruwell, who refused to give up on anyone. I think having something hopeful and life-giving to move toward makes a world of difference.

Q *Why was writing so powerful for Maria and the other Freedom Writers?*

A They got to experience why writing is such a powerful tool, shield, and weapon. It allows people to tell their own story, not have it told "at them" by outsiders. By reading and meeting other writers, they also experienced their common humanity with people from very different cultures. By the way, *all* of the real-life Freedom Writers graduated from high school, and many went on to college.

What to Read Next

Fiction

Drive-By, Lynne Ewing. (96 pages) *Tito's older brother is killed in a drive-by shooting, and then the whole family is in danger.*

Holes, Louis Sachar. (272 pages) *Stanley Yelnats was in the wrong place at the wrong time, and now he's in a juvenile detention center unlike any other.*

Jumped, Rita William-Garcia. (192 pages) *Three high school girls are involved in what may turn out to be a really ugly fight.*

The Juvie Three, Gordon Korman. (256 pages) *Three teenage boys in juvie get a last chance to avoid being locked up.*

Miracle's Boys, Jacqueline Woodson. (160 pages) *Lafayette is raised by his two teenage brothers after his mother and father die.*

The Outsiders, S. E. Hinton. (192 pages) *Ponyboy and his friends are in constant battle with kids from the other side of town.*

The Skin I'm In, Sharon Flake. (176 pages) *Maleeka is having a tough time in middle school, but she gets unexpected help from a new teacher.*

Scorpions, Walter Dean Myers. (224 pages) *A 13-year-old boy's life changes drastically after he is pressured to become the leader of a gang.*

Nonfiction

The Diary of a Young Girl, Anne Frank. (304 pages) *Anne Frank kept this diary while she and her family were in hiding from the Nazis during World War II.*

Gifted Hands, Kids Edition, Ben Carson. (144 pages) *This is the story of how Ben Carson escaped poverty and the mean streets of Detroit and became one of the world's best neurosurgeons.*

Voices from the Street: Young Former Gang Members Tell Their Stories, S. Beth Atkin. (131 pages) *Girls and boys who have quit gangs describe their experiences.*

For More Info

Books
The Freedom Writers Diary: How a Teacher and 150 Teens Used Writing to Change Themselves and the World Around Them, with Erin Gruwell. (292 pages) *The Freedom Writers and Erin Gruwell tell how hard work and courage can change lives.*

The Other Wes Moore: One Name, Two Fates, Wes Moore. (272 pages) *Wes Moore's best-selling memoir examines the paths that he and the other Wes Moore took.*

The Pact: Three Young Men Make a Promise and Fulfill a Dream, Sampson Davis, George Jenkins, Rameck Hunt, and Liza Frazier Page. (272 pages) *Three black teenagers from Newark, New Jersey, make a pact to go to college and become doctors.*

Films and Videos
Freedom Writers (2007) *This film tells the story of Erin Gruwell and the Freedom Writers.*

Websites
www.freedomwritersfoundation.org
This site for the foundation started by Erin Gruwell and her students provides stories, advice, and ways to get involved.

www.homeboy-industries.org
This site is for an organization started by Father Greg Boyle to help keep young people out of prison by providing them support, job placement, and education.

Glossary

ankle monitor (ANG-kuhl MON-uh-tur) *noun* a device that allows the police to track the location of a person under house arrest

barrio (BA-ree-oh) *noun* a neighborhood in a U.S. city where Spanish is the main language

carjacking (KAR-jak-ing) *noun* the theft of a vehicle by force

chica (CHEE-kah) *noun* a girl, in Spanish. In this book, the term refers to a Latin American female gang member.

cholo (CHOH-lo) *noun* a term used to refer to a male member of a Latino gang

colors (KUHL-urz) *noun* in this book, clothing in a color that shows membership in a particular gang

drive-by (DRIVE-bye) *noun* a shooting done from a moving vehicle

GED (JEE EE DEE) *noun* short for General Educational Development, a test given to determine that someone has reached a level equivalent to having graduated from high school

Holocaust (HOL-uh-kost) *noun* the mass murder of six million Jews by the Nazis during World War II

Islam (i-SLAHM) *noun* the religion based on the teachings of the Koran, a book that Muslims accept as the word of Allah as told to the prophet Muhammad

juvenile detention center (JOO-vuh-nile di-TEN-shuhn SEN-tur) *noun* a jail to hold young people until they are taken to court or sent to a long-term prison

Nazi (NOT-see) *noun* a member of the group, led by Adolf Hitler, that ruled Germany from 1933 to 1945

obituary (oh-BIT-choo-er-ee) *noun* a notice of a person's death, often with a short account of the person's life

probation (proh-BAY-shuhn) *noun* an agreement to release a person convicted of a crime from prison for as long as he or she displays good behavior while under close supervision

row house (ROH HOUSS) *noun* a house joined to another by a shared wall

shank (SHANK) *verb* slang for to stab with a homemade knife

tolerance (TOL-ur-uhnss) *noun* the willingness to respect or accept the customs, beliefs, or opinions of others

veteranos (vet-uhr-AH-noze) *noun* longtime members of a Latino gang

Sources

MOMENT OF TRUTH

The Other Wes Moore: One Name, Two Fates, Wes Moore. New York: Spiegel & Garu, 2010. (including quotes on pages 4, 13, 15, 23, 33, 49, 50, 53)

Author's interview with Wes Moore in 2011. (including quote on page 49)

"Books: Author Wes Moore." *Charlie Rose*, June 4, 2010. (including quotes on pages 16, 31)

"The Destinies of Two Men Who Share One Name," Michele Norris. NPR's *All Things Considered*, April 28, 2010.

"Five Cornerstones," Valley Forge Military Academy and College website.

"Hopkins Senior a Rhodes Scholar," Laura Cadiz. *Baltimore Sun*, December 11, 2000. (including quote on page 21)

"In Honor of Fallen Heroes," Nancy A. Youssef. *Baltimore Sun*, May 6, 2000. (including quote on page 47)

JobCorps.gov Job Corps official website

"*The Other Wes Moore* Author Knows What Might Have Been," Deirdre Donahue. *USA Today*, May 7, 2010. (including quote on page 52)

"The Other Wes Moore: The Felon and the Rhodes Scholar," Thomas Rogers. Salon.com, May 9, 2010. (including quote on page 42)

"Read Street: Q&A with Author Wes Moore, *The Other Wes Moore*," Michael Sragow. *Baltimore Sun*, April 29, 2010. (including quote on page 32)

"Same Name, Different Fate." Oprah.com, April 27, 2010. (including quotes on pages 21, 23, 51)

"Two Wanted in Officer's Killing Are Captured in Philadelphia," Dan Thanh Dang. *Baltimore Sun*, February 20, 2000. (including quote on page 20)

BIRD IN A CAGE

Author's interview with Maria Reyes in 2010. (including quotes on pages 60, 61, 67, 91–92, 96–97)

The Freedom Writers Diary: How a Teacher and 150 Teens Used Writing to Change Themselves and the World Around Them, the Freedom Writers with Erin Gruwell. New York: Random House, 1999. (including quotes on pages 62, 85, 93, 95–96)

"California Juvenile Justice System Facts," Youth Law Center, August 2009.

"'Freedom Writer' Brings Inspiring Message to Chesterfield High School," Juan Antonio Lizama. *Richmond Times-Dispatch,* October 16, 2009.

"'Freedom Writer' Maria Reyes Inspires Mona Shores Middle School Students," Teresa Taylor Williams. *Muskegon Chronicle,* March 13, 2009.

"Freedom Writer: Woman Shows How At-Risk Kids Can Succeed," Sandy Meindersma. *Worcester Telegram & Gazette,* November 22, 2009.

"Gruwell, Founder of Freedom Writers, Speaks to Students about Experiences Teaching Inner City Students," Apsara Iyer. *Phillipian,* October 21, 2010.

"I Escaped a Violent Gang," Cate Baily. *Scholastic Scope,* February 8, 1999. (including quotes on pages 5, 73, 96)

"Interview with Maria." Scholastic 2009 National Advisory Council DVD. (including quote on page 90)

"Maria Reyes, Co-Author of *The Freedom Writers Diary,* Speaks on the Importance of Teachers and Education." Marymount University, November 18, 2010.

"Maria Reyes, Freedom Writer." Milwaukee Teachers' Education Association.

"Pen Is Mightier than the Sword in Erin Gruwell's Class." Utah Education Association, December 2007.

Teaching Hope: Stories from the Freedom Writer Teachers and Erin Gruwell, Erin Gruwell and her students. New York: Broadway Books, 2009. (including quotes on pages 82–83)

"A True Freedom Writer," Maria Reyes. Posted on YouTube.com, May 2010. (including quotes on pages 64, 67, 76–77, 84, 88)

Index